T0298301

To Pause at the Threshold

Reflections on Living on the Border

Esther de Waal

Morehouse Publishing
NEW YORK · HARRISBURG · DENVER

First published in 2001 as *Living on the Border: Connecting Inner and Outer Worlds* by The Canterbury Press Norwich (a publishing imprint of Hymns Ancient & Modern Limited, a registered charity), St Mary's Works, St Mary's Plain, Norwich, Norfolk NR3 3BH.

First North American edition published 2004 by Morehouse Publishing, 4775 Linglestown Road, Harrisburg, Pennsylvania 17112. American edition revised and expanded.

Morehouse Publishing is an imprint of Church Publishing Incorporated.

www.churchpublishing.org

Cover art: Timoleague Abbey, Timoleague, Ireland © Richard Cummins/ Superstock, Inc.

Design by Corey Kent

Library of Congress Cataloging-in-Publication Data

De Waal, Esther.
  To pause at the threshold: reflections on living on the border / Esther de Waal.
       p. cm. Includes bibliographical references (p. 95).
ISBN 978-0-8192-1989-3 (pbk.)
  1. Spiritual life—Anglican Communion. 2. De Waal, Esther I. Title.
  BV4501.3.D44 2004
  283'.092—dc22

                              2003022866

For
the Brothers of the Order of the Holy Cross,
who have crossed many thresholds
and encouraged others
to do the same

Contents

Introduction

There is a traditional saying of ancient wisdom: "A threshold is a sacred thing." In some places of the world, in some traditional cultures, and in monastic life, this is still remembered. It is something, however, that we generally forget today, and I would count myself among those who do not always find it easy to remember. But it is something that I have deliberately been attempting to recover for myself, and which I now want to share. I hope this book encourages others to take time to pause at the threshold.

When I visited Japan I experienced the role of the threshold in a very simple daily experience. Before entering the house, the Japanese stand on the lintel in order to remove the shoes worn outside in the street. Upon entering the house, they put on slippers placed inside the door. This forces a very deliberate and conscious way of standing still, even if for only a moment, in order to show respect for the difference between two spaces, the outer and the inner; the preparation for the encounter with another person, another household.

This is very similar to the traditional monastic practice of *statio*, which also pays homage to the threshold moment, and shows reverence for the handling of space and time. The monk or nun enters the church for the saying of the daily offices, but always leaves him- or herself time to stand, to wait, to let go of all the demands of whatever the previous activity had been, with all its concurrent anxieties and expectations. That stillness permits each one to enter into that space kept empty in the heart for the Word of God. By rushing, whether through a sense of duty or obligation, or to save a few extra moments for the task at hand, they may gain something in terms of daily work. What is lost, however, is the attention, the awareness of the crossing over into the time and the place for *opus Dei*, the work of God.

Discovering the traditional practices of the Celtic peoples, as they have come down by word of mouth, has shown me how hard-working and demanding lives can still be shaped by time taken to recognize and to rejoice in the succession of times of change, in each day, in every season year by year, in the pattern of life itself from birth to death. The Celts had their rituals and their celebrations for acknowledging these times of change, and I have included them in this book, for I myself have gained so much from trying to incorporate them into my own life. But I also feel that there are wider implications here for the way that we address our public lives, in all the inescapable issues in church, in politics, and the world situation.

I have written elsewhere about learning to see with wonder and delight, about mystery, about the amazing universe that opens up for me when I look at a flower or a stone through a magnifying glass.[1] But I want now to take as my starting point what I have received from the landscape around my home, the countryside where I grew up and where I have now returned to live, the border country between England and Wales. At this stage of my life, I am setting out to uncover—though it might be better to speak of it as to recover or to rediscover—it in such a way that the exterior landscape may shape and mold the interior landscape.

For I am not writing just about a rural situation of great beauty, with a history stretching far back into time. In this book I want to read a landscape so that it reveals itself and gives an image of God at work in his world. Above all I want to explore the role of thresholds, of the crossing-over places, not only geographical ones but also metaphorical thresholds. I have found that these same thresholds have been explored by a writer growing up in totally different circumstances from my own who described how, as a young boy, he realized the significance of belonging to two worlds. His growing up in these two worlds sharpened his perception so that he later saw it as a formative experience.

The twentieth-century English novelist Graham Greene wrote a travel book in which he gave the subtitle "Across the River" to his opening chapter "The Border," in spite of the fact that his journey lay across dry land without any water—neither river nor sea—in the vicinity. And that at once reminds us of the role of the image and the part that it is bound to play in the exploration of crossing-over, boundaries, thresholds—the theme I wish to explore in this small book.

All our lives are inevitably made of a succession of borders and thresholds, which open up into the new and promise excitement or fear. The traveler encountering unknown places has all the exhilaration, the thrill of another country. Graham Greene writes vividly of the expectancy waiting on the further side:

> Over there everything is going to be different; life is never going to be quite the same again after your passport has been stamped and you find yourself speechless among the money-changers. The man seeking scenery imagines stranger woods and unheard-of mountains; the romantic believes that the women over the border will be more beautiful and complaisant than those at home; the unhappy man imagines at least a different hell; the suicidal traveller expects the death he never finds. The atmosphere

of the border—it is like starting over again, there is something about it like a good confession. . . .[2]

This passage is about a geographical border between two countries. But from his early childhood Greene knew the juxtaposition of two metaphorical countries, for his home was part of a large boarding school and he had only to open a door to move between two worlds: one smelling of books and fruit and eau de cologne, and the other of damp towels and ink and disinfectant. Sometimes he lived surrounded by a gentle croquet lawn, with flowerbeds and raspberry canes, and at other times by great square buildings of harsh brick, stone stairs, and cracked bells. He was an inhabitant of both countries, sometimes on one side of the door and sometimes on the other. Pulled by these different ties he asked: "How can life on a border be other than restless?"

I, too, have lived in more than one world. I have come back to live where I grew up. I have returned to the slower rhythms and the earth-linked textures of life on the Welsh Borders. Life here is a total contrast to the years spent elsewhere, in a big university in the Midlands or an important cathedral city in the crowded southeast of England. As I root myself here I am finding that it is at once familiar and strange. This landscape has become my teacher, my mentor.

It takes time to recognize this, but I am beginning to realize just how profound an effect it has had on my life, on the way that I approach time, people, situations, and issues. I suppose that I might sum it up by saying that I have become aware of the continual movement of crossing over thresholds into the new, while still of course being part of what is left behind. It applies above all in my own life and in the emerging pattern that I discern now that I am (as my journalist son put it so magnificently) on the cusp of old age. But it has also influenced the way in which I look at situations and how I relate to other people. As I try to sum it up, a whole galaxy of words starts to come tumbling out: openness to change, ready and willing to move forward, living without defenses rather than hiding behind barriers. In the end, if I were to find one single word that catches this sense of thresholds opening up what is new and unknown, it would be *transformation*—and transformations, as L. William Countryman reminds

us, "are always at least a little scary." To be transformed implies letting go of control for a while
in the hopeful expectation that something worth-
while may result. It means taking the risk that
old certainties might be replaced by a new way of
seeing the world. Another word is *conversion,* not
in the relatively easy sense of changing to religion,
or from one denomination to another, but in the
much more demanding sense of "turning round,"
and "discovering that there's a whole world out
there that you hadn't really been aware of."[3]

I can only learn from this border countryside
landscape when I let its presence reveal itself to me
gently, so that I begin to sense its patterns—those
hill rhythms and water rhythms that had such a
profound effect upon David Jones, the artist and
poet, when he lived a few miles away at Capel-y-ffin
in the Llanthony valley in the Black Mountains.
In an autobiographical talk he said that in those
years between 1924 and 1926, as he came to know
the valley and the hills, he found that his work
was influenced by the strong hill rhythms and the
bright counter-rhythms of the water brooks. He
found that there was no stillness in this landscape,
but that here the movement of streams, wind, rain,

and clouds ceaselessly transformed—in change that reveals the unchanging.[4]

Already I am being brought into a world where significant things are shown as images, and insight comes from shapes and patterns, from the visual rather than from the written word. Here I come face to face with what is elemental, both in my own self and in the world around. So although I began with the experience of a physical landscape I have been taken beyond that to explore successively the interplay of light and dark, of time and season, as they alternate and move on, and my own life as it also moves forward. I consider how I am to embrace change in the context of the movement from birth to death, with its universal and inescapable stages. Am I willing to cross the threshold of new understanding by being open and receptive, not closed in and defensive? These questions also arise as I think not only about physical growth but also about growth into understanding and wisdom. The most profound threshold, however, remains that between the inner and the outer, between going deeper into the interior self and emerging to meet the world beyond the self without protective defenses, as friend not as foe.

How can a life on the border be other than rest-less, as Graham Greene wrote? That is one of the questions that I want to address. I feel, and I guess I am not alone in this, that more and more of us are finding ourselves in a place where two worlds meet, and I ask, "How do I hold this together? How do I make this a creative encounter? How do I stop myself from being pulled in one direction or the other?" There seems to be no easy or obvious answer to these questions. But I see that moment of crossing over as the threshold moment, the pause between, and this I believe is what holds the key to what I hope to explore.

I

The Border Landscape

Reading a landscape

I am now setting out to uncover or rediscover a whole world that lies around me, and to discover it in such a way that the outer landscape might shape and mold the inner landscape. It is an exploration that I believe I can best undertake by using the imagination in image and poetry and metaphor.

As I turn to the land and to its poets and artists, I want to make this an undertaking not only for myself. I hope that my own specific encounter with a specific place may also speak to my readers and give them images that they can relate to their own personal experiences. This book comes out of a particular place that I know, but it is ultimately about making any place or any circumstance the threshold into the other, the new, the strange, and showing the image of difference, mystery, otherness at work in God's world.

Although my earliest childhood was spent in the Welsh border countryside, I was never taught to read the landscape around me. I did not ask questions about it, for neither did my father. He was an antiquarian of the old school and I owe him my sense of history and my knowledge of medieval architecture. His approach was quintessentially that of a man fascinated by factual information of a most precise nature. He wanted to be able to date stones, whether in their natural state or shaped and used by local builders, but these were not living stones: they did not cry out. This was a world on which categories and labels were imposed, a world known through charts and charters, dates and land grants. These land charters, with their concern for the giving and transferring of land between one owner and another, between one estate and another, encouraged an attitude of certainty and clarity about the past.

From my mother I learned another sort of certainty: certainty about the present, for she held very clear ideas about our neighbors across the border in Wales. Prejudice simplified her approach: the Welsh were small in stature, unreliable in character, not to be trusted, and unworthy of any respect. "Taffy was a Welshman, Taffy was a thief," the old jingle tripped only too easily off the tongue. They came to raid, crossing over into England to make inroads into our fair and pleasant land. Therefore, there was not any idea of giving and receiving, and doorways were shut, defrauding me of what, even as a small child, might have taught me to be receptive, ready to learn from the other. I had no sense of thresholds to cross, or borders to break; there was nothing to encourage openness or exploration.

Living on the border

But as so often happens in life, I was given a second chance. When I was married and with four young sons, my father presented us with a small cottage— two rooms upstairs and two rooms downstairs, the traditional local pattern, with only one cold water tap and no inside lavatory. Two streams meet here, the Cwm and the Greidol, and flow over into a waterfall, where at the base lies a mass of huge rock slabs whose shape and position would gradually but dramatically change over the years under the impact of flood and storm. These swirling combinations of mud and silt and stone, continually different and new, gave me a metaphor for a natural configuration that maintains its essential form while retaining its ability to shape and adapt over the years. Since time immemorial, streams have formed the boundaries between properties and settlements and very often, as here, they still carry their earliest Celtic or Welsh names. But even though the streams' names might be Welsh, the village name was Saxon and politically part of England, even while the church is still the proud possessor of the Great Welsh Bible, the first Bible

to be translated into Welsh by William Morgan
in 1588. A mile or two away, the neighboring tiny
church of Llangua—which can date its origins
to a sixth-century Celtic saint—lies geographi-
cally in Wales while yet remaining in the Church
of England. Any neat demarcation, whether religious, economic, or cultural, has little meaning in
a border countryside such as this.

So when I went walking along the stretch of
Offa's Dyke that ran only a few miles away, I came
to know afresh the world that had earlier delighted
my father. He had told me the heroic story of Offa
and his eighth-century ambitions, the man who
dominated the whole of Britain between *757* and
795, a contemporary and almost an equal of the
emperor Charlemagne. But that was now something of the historic past. A military frontier had
become a pastoral border, though with visible
differences whose pattern one could see written on
the land itself. It was still a place where two worlds
met. I felt that I was looking beyond political
ambition and military conquest. Of course I could
see those differences: they were written into the
pattern of the landscape. There was Wales on the
west side, a country of mountains and scattered

settlements, bare stretches of hillside covered with sheep and wild ponies. I recalled David Jones's delight in the legend that these were the descendants of the horses of Arthur's knights, when they ran free after the defeat of the king and the end of Arthurian Britain. Now shrunk in size "those straying riderless horses gone to grass in forest and on mountain, seem, as their masters, to have acquired a new yet aboriginal liberty."[1] On the east side, in contrast, lay a rolling landscape of low hills and prosperous farms where neat hedgerows enclosed fields that were the result of the more fertile soil and the strength of the landowning families. Two different worlds met here, each with its own past, shaped by geography, politics, and people.

Through others' eyes

So as I live here once again I am presented by the simple reality of the land. It is my mentor, my teacher, and in it I have a guide who can never become theoretical or abstract, for I am learning the wisdom of the earth itself, the ground beneath my feet, the people who settled it and shaped its cultivation. Above all, living deep in the countryside, I am faced with what I could so easily be unaware of in a city: the alternation of light and dark, the changing patterns of the seasons and the years, the ebb and flow of solstice and equinox.

As I return to live here, I find a place, a situation, that is both familiar and mysterious. That is right. It should take time for something to reveal itself, to unveil its meaning. Many of us were struck by the way in which, when he was asked a question during a radio interview, Archbishop Rowan Williams said, "May I take a moment?" For many of us who were listening, accustomed as we had become to the cut and thrust of the quick question and the immediate response in public discussion, this was a defining moment. It reminded us just how important it is to pause, in this as in any other context. It is to recall the role of reverence and respect, in a question, in another person, in a situation.

This is what I have gained from my encounter with my native landscape. In the end, this border country and what it brings must remain elusive, like the mists and the ever-changing colors. It will speak to each of us differently, and it will say different things to us at different times. It will strike chords and bring glimpses. It may also bring gifts of sudden insight. But it can never be possessed or fully understood. All of this is a reason for great gratitude.

The landscape, as David Jones reminds me, also points me to an awareness of movement, change, and ceaseless transformation. If I were to try to sum it up very simply, I would say that it has made me aware of continual movement, crossing over thresholds while yet remaining firmly rooted in this place where I still belong. So at once I realize that I am in a situation that is not sheltered and safe, for to be transformed means being open, and while standing firmly in this place where I belong, I am firmly rooted yet never static.

R. S. Thomas, the Welsh poet *par excellence* of our day, is also, in effect, speaking of the importance of being hesitant at the threshold, when he holds out this warning to those who have become too possessive of what they see of his native country:

> You can come in
> You can come a long way . . .
> But you won't be inside.[2]

This encounter with place is such a personal experience that it is not surprising to find that the one thing all writers, whether of prose or poetry, have in common is that they respect the way in which landscape opens up depths beyond itself. Bonnie Thurston, an American poet and theologian who has come to know and love the Welsh Borders, brings her own particular vision of the land:

> On a glorious summer day
> this border country rolls out
> in a carpet of green turf,
> the fertile result
> of a blood-soaked history.
> A place where armies marched,
> kings were made and broken . . . .
>
> Border lands often murmur
> of what was and might have been.
> God draws back the veil
> to make a Golden Valley
> between the Black Mountains,
> a place teeming with the life of
> presence and past.[3]

There is great gentleness and hope in these lines. The past is there with its memories of battle and death, and there is blood-soaked land, but there is also fertility, the green turf that has sprung from the destruction. Above all there is the Golden Valley with all the promise that its name inspires. As God draws back the veil we see how this landscape sings. Here is the good news: different cultures and stories meet and mix, they challenge one another, and from their meeting the new can flourish.

Border or frontier?

By a strange irony there is a place I visit frequently and with which I have a strong connection that allows me to measure the strength of and appreciate the gift that I receive at home more fully. As I was thinking about the theme of this small book, I spent three months in a Benedictine monastery in South Africa, uMariya uMama weThemba, founded by the American Episcopalian Order of the Holy Cross. This became particularly significant, for I found that I was now beginning to ask myself questions: What is a frontier? A border? A

boundary? A threshold? A boundary gives a necessary definition—a structure, a framework that
one respects. The whole monastic life shows us the
vital role of that—boundaries of time and place,
held in a flexible rhythm that brings order and
certainty, and with this comes freedom (as it does
of course in the parallel situation of the family[4]).
Boundaries, any good psychologist will tell us
(and the monastic tradition has an excellent grasp
of psychological insight), are very important and
must be respected. A frontier, however, is designed
to exclude the other. It is the product of hostil-
ity, aggression, and power. But my experience
is of the Welsh Marches, neither boundary nor
frontier, but a borderland that marks (where of
course the old term Marches or Marcher Lords
originates) the point where the lands of two peoples
run alongside one another. So I see borderlands
as places where different cultures and histories
meet and mix, perhaps challenge one another, and
from which the new can then open up. And what
I find in this outer landscape (which is my home)
has also become true of that inner landscape, the
inscape, which I cultivate and nurture.

In the eastern Cape in South Africa, I was able to see a complete contrast in the way an imperial power had established frontiers to keep peoples apart. In order to push the Xhosa people back beyond the great Fish River, the British created a network of fortified positions along a line marked by palisades and forts, manned by constant patrols intended to maintain "a proper degree of terror." Here was a deliberate policy of creating barriers in order to establish a clear demarcation line between cultural and racial difference, white and black, by excluding and dividing. First written, as it were, on the soil itself in the nineteenth century, it was next to be carried over into legal, social, and economic spheres in the twentieth century under the regime of apartheid. The white proponents of that regime were so completely and utterly confident of the Tightness of their stance that they shut the door totally on the other. Metaphorically, they barricaded themselves into their *laagers,* those circles of upturned wagons that the Afrikaners traditionally used to protect themselves on their long marches. Two worlds had now become polarized, without contact, without sympathy or understanding.

A border priory

In the Welsh Marches I realized with gratitude that I belonged to a world where both landscape and buildings gave me another message. St. Mary's Priory in Monmouth, a few miles from my home, is a border place in every sense. It tells a wonderful story of how cultures and peoples have met and mingled there. We find a Benedictine priory built in Wales after the Norman Conquest, a daughter house founded from a mother house in the Loire Valley in France, but also having a Breton involvement, which introduces a Celtic element. In the preface to the history of the priory church, Rowan Williams, then the Archbishop of Wales and bishop of Monmouth explores the full significance of such a border situation:

> This history gives us a good metaphor for a central aspect of Christian ministry. The priory built on a past legacy but moved in a new direction; it was founded by strangers who were also kindred. It is a "border" place in every sense; and the future of the priory buildings must be about how that border is

explored in such a way as to change strangers into kindred, and to bring people closer to that dangerous and transforming border between the world and God—the border that God himself upsets by his entry into the world on our terms, in flesh and blood.

Across the border, then, whether it's a human border or the strange frontier with God, is something or someone who is more hospitable than we dreamed; and we learn this by taking the risk of hospitality ourselves. Benedictine life is centered on God and on guests, seeing each in the other and learning from each how to relate to the other.[5]

Interlude:
Standing on the Threshold

Rowan Williams tells us to take the risk of hospitality. When we turn to the Rule of St. Benedict, we are shown the fullness of what hospitality can mean. It is not merely the open door or the open gate that offers warmth, food, and drink, but also the open heart offering acceptance and love, and not least the open mind ready and willing to listen and to receive and exchange. St. Benedict tells us to give a welcome to all who come because we see in them the figure of Christ himself. This means not judging or labeling, not being critical or competitive, not imprisoning the other in our demands and expectations. As he so often does, St. Benedict presents profound theological teaching in very down-to-earth and immediate terms. In Chapter 62 he describes the porter who stands at the gate of the monastery to exercise this art of hospitality on behalf of his brothers.

It is tender, funny, and wise, a very simple but profound portrait, and we should not overlook its implications as a model for any of us. We see a man on the threshold, with one foot, as it were, in the monastic enclosure and the other in the world outside. Whenever anyone appears, he calls out his greeting *"Deo Gratias"* "Thank God you have come." It is a real welcome, of loving openness, and St. Benedict uses two very simple phrases to describe it: "all the gentleness that comes from the fear of God" and "the warmth of love."

In my own thinking and praying I have extended the image of the man on the margin to include the greeting of new circumstances, new situations, and new demands, so that even when they appear unexpectedly and I feel unready and ill equipped, I am yet prepared to welcome them. This image of being simultaneously rooted yet open, planted on either side of the threshold of the interior and the exterior, is one that I now want to apply elsewhere in my own personal experience.

2

Times and Seasons or Crossing Between Light and Dark

Place and time are the two primordial, inescapable realities that can either imprison or liberate us. How do we handle them? Even recognizing this and realizing that it is our responsibility can be the first step to freedom. I find that I have been given an unexpected image in the form of the medieval chained library of Hereford cathedral, and as the priest-poet David Scott reminds us, if we are thinking of heaven and earth—"two major and distinct realities and you want to build some sort of bridge between them"—then we can only deal in images that have always been tools for writers for the exploration of truths.[1] In Hereford cathedral we find the Mappa Mundi, which is not actually a map in the usual sense but instead, in an apparently geographical map, gives us a picture of the medieval understanding of the world. Jerusalem is placed at the center, surrounded by countries and creatures, true or fantastical, which make up a total universe, real and imaginary, human and non-human, and in the triangular apex above the round world is Christ in Majesty presiding over it all, the work of his creation and redemption. We see God seated in glory and in judgment, inside and outside of time. And so here I am given an image of another border: that between time and eternity.[2]

For many of us, time has become yet one more commodity of the consumer world, a commodity at the mercy of the dictates of deadlines and contracts, valued in terms of achievement and productivity. It is not easy to regain a sense of the changes of time and season when the night sky with all its gentle and subtle changes is blotted out by the sullen orange glow of the sodium light, denying us what should rightly be the timeless heritage of the movement of moon and stars. When the imported luxuries of the world stare us in the face on every visit to the supermarket, we are denied any sense of the coming and going of successive seasons of the year, with the expectation and delight that each will bring its own particular gift. If the kiwi fruits and the tomatoes and the strawberries are endlessly available, there is no longer that waiting on the threshold for each new season to bring its appropriate contribution of fruitfulness.

Yet living here I cannot fail to be aware of movement, the movement of water, of light and dark, of the coming and going of each season in turn, and with it the underlying theme of ebb and flow, of death and life, the dying down of nature and the new seed of creation and re-creation, experienced again and again, year in year out, just as it will be repeated time and again throughout our lives. It demands active response, involvement. I remember hearing that Parker Palmer was once told about what to expect from an upper mid-west winter: "The winters will drive you crazy until you learn to get out into them."

In an attempt to remember, to recall, to live with these as gifts, to handle light and dark, time and season with respect and reverence, I have begun in recent years to look at the annual pattern of the changeover of the days and the seasons as the Celtic peoples of the Scottish islands used to do. I have made a commitment to incorporate into my own life the riches of the Celtic oral tradition that has come down to us from generation to generation and shows us so vividly their way of looking at the world. Of course in my case it applies very easily since I also live in a northern clime, but it is the underlying approach and attitude that I want to encourage people to discover and use for themselves, in their own terms.

Every day each of us experiences that alternation between night and day as we move between dawn and dusk, between being asleep and awake. After all, life is shaped by this regular border movement written into daily life in an inescapable pattern of crossing over between the two. Both the light and the dark have always captured the imagination

of writers and poets, of theologians, of all early
peoples living close to the land. When I came upon
these words from a Christmas sermon by St. Leo
the Great, the fifth-century pope, I wondered, as I
have wondered so often, why we neglect the riches
of our great Christian tradition, and as a result do
not use the glorious energy in a passage such as
this:

> O man [and woman] rouse yourself!
> Learn to know the dignity of your nature.
>
> . . .
>
> Use this visible creation as it should be used,
> as you use the earth, sea, sky, air, springs and rivers;
> and whatever is beautiful and wonderful
> in them acknowledging the praise and glory of God.
>
> Touch the physical light with the bodily sense
> and embrace with all the power of your soul
> that true light . . .[3]

Naturally the coming of the light had practical
consequences that inspired the daily rituals we
find among the Celtic peoples, since the coming of
morning light, and the cessation of that light each

night, governed their life and work. It is important
that, as we read these prayers and blessings today,
we put them into the context of gaining a liveli-
hood in circumstances that were harsh, unroman-
tic, and unsafe, a world that demanded courage.
Ritual brought a sense of order into what they did,
and connected them with the reality of time and
season.

The pattern of the day

Living on the borders brings me a very clear sense
of the movement of time—of light and dark, of
the changing seasons—and with it the underlying themes of death and life, darkness and light,
creation and re-creation, inescapable for any of us
whether we live in an urban or a rural environment.
For here we find ourselves touched by something
primal, that repetition of birth and death, dying
and new life, experienced again and again, year in
and year out, repeated throughout our lives.

The Celtic world had rituals for every day and
every season, so the passage of time was marked
with due reverence and awareness. The day would
start by saluting the rising sun, whom they hailed

as they would a great person returning to their land. When the sun rose over the tops of the peaks, an old man in Arisaig would remove his head-covering and bow his head down, giving glory to the great God of life for the magnificence of the sun and for the goodness of its light to the children of men and to the animals of the world.

> Hail to thee, thou sun of the seasons,
> As thou traversest the skies aloft,
> Thy steps are strong on the wing of the heavens.[4]

Inside the house the woman lays the foundation of her domestic duties by spreading the embers of the fire, which has been burning throughout the night, in three equal sections in a circle, putting a peat between them so that each will touch the small boss in the middle that forms the common center. The first peat is laid down in the name of the God of Life, the second in the name of the God of Peace, the third in the name of the God of Grace, and the circle is then covered in the name of the Three of Light. Fire, light, warmth—the image of the nurturing and sustaining hand of God and of the need for these same qualities within our own selves, is here enacted as a daily ritual. This custom can easily seem romantic and distant, far removed from the technology of the electric switch, the automatic coffee maker, the electric kettle, or whatever forms the first ritual of bringing warmth into the start of our day. And yet the reality of performing an action with awareness, consciousness of the presence of God, gratitude for his gifts of power or water or light, still remains the same. An action undertaken consciously and with reverence gives meaning to the start of the day and thus to a hallowing of time and its handling with care.

In the Celtic tradition, this daily celebration of the coming of the light of each day then became a daily reminder of heaven, of the future light of eternity:

> O God, who broughtest me from the rest of last night
> Unto the joyous light of this day,
> Be Thou bringing me from the new light of this day
> Unto the guiding light of eternity.
> Oh! from the new light of this day
> Unto the guiding light of eternity.

Then there is a prayer in the evening, as the light fades at dusk, at the time of "the change-over routine," as naturalists in Africa call that moment when evening falls and the wild creatures welcome the coming of the darkness.

> I am in hope, in its proper time,
> That the great and gracious God
> Will not put out for me the light of grace
> Even as thou dost leave me this night.

This is a reminder of something that is only too easy to forget in a culture of urban values: both the light and the dark have a role to play. John Davies, a bishop who has known both Africa and England, and who now lives on the borders in North Wales reminds us: "There is a place within the providence of God for the darkness, the night, the shadow. Our individual formation is in the dark, between conception and birth. The mysterious workings of our bodies are in the dark. The seed grows secretly in the dark. . . . We need to recognise and work with this darkness, even when we feel that it is opposing the light which is the primary gift of God."[5]

"Darkness and light are both alike to Thee," sings the psalmist, and just as we can learn so much from the songs of the people of Israel, so we also

learn from the songs that were always in the hearts
and on the lips of the Celtic peoples. They make
me conscious of what otherwise I might easily
neglect, those crossing-over moments that carry
me between the dark and the light, the light and
the dark, taking me daily and yearly from one to
the other.

> The eye of the great God
> The eye of the God of glory,
> The eye of the King of hosts,
> The eye of the King of the living,
> Pouring upon us
> At each time and season
> Pouring upon us
> Gently and generously.

There are so many prayers throughout the ages
on the celebration of the coming of the light—the
light that is the dawn, that is the light of life, that
is Christ himself. I end this section with one that
I have taken from Bede, so that if we turn to the
Celtic tradition we do not forget the riches of the
Anglo-Saxon world:

Grant us your light, O Lord,
that the darkness in our hearts
being wholly passed away,
we may come at last to the light
which is Christ.
For Christ is the morning star,
who when the night of this world has passed,
brings to us
the promised light of life,
and opens to them eternal day. Amen.[6]

Praying the seasons

In recent years I have begun quite consciously to live the pattern of time in the Celtic way and it has given me much joy because now I value change as I never did before. What I most appreciate is that four times in each year there is a pause, a festival, a named day, marking the transitional moment between one season and the next. For as the sun annually passed through its four stations, the equinoxes and the solstices became significant moments of the year. They were celebrated as a succession of threshold moments, each with its name and its rituals to carry men and women forward to the next season.

The year began at Samhaine on November 1. Country folk around me still speak of this as "the turning of the year," and for many people, whether they celebrate the pre-Christian Samhaine or the Christian feasts of All Saints and All Souls, this is the thinnest time of the year, the time at which the veil between time and eternity can easily become transparent. With the drawing in of the days, the coming of darkness, and the prospect of winter with all its attendant hardships and ills, this was the time to bring the flocks down from their summer pastures, and those animals that could not be kept would be slaughtered and their carcasses and bones burnt in bonfires. In the words of the twentieth-century poet of the Hebrides George Mackay Brown, it was as if "the children of the sun were entreating the light to return from darkness, to stay with them, to provide them with corn and milk and fleeces through the lessening days of autumn and winter."[7] The landscape becomes bare, stripped, cold, stark, dead.

Can we still find significance in the passing of the seasons? Can we live into them in such a way that we allow their changes to shape the pattern of our prayer? It is undoubtedly easier in a place where I can watch the moon wax and wane, see the stars move across the horizon, see the trees gain and lose their foliage, and notice the gradual shading of the colors around me. To begin the year with the drawing in of the days from November 1, which I have now begun to do, has become significant and powerful in my own life. It must inevitably take a different form in a town, but if you look you can still try to find the images that encourage turning the cycle of the seasons into reflective praying.

Fr. Philip Jebb, OSB, Prior of the Benedictine Abbey of Downside, has given us his own response:

Winter has a message all its own;

. . .

The trees are naked, without leaves or flowers or fruit;
But the bare branches give us glimpses of the stars;
They reach their fingers to heaven,
Even as their roots hold fast to the earth.
Linked by the strong trunk, giving interchange of life,
symbols of our dual nature and inheritance.[8]

Spring comes with the feast of Imboic on February 1 (which is also the feast of St. Brigid, and the following day is Candlemas). This is the time of the lactation of the ewes, and for those of us in the northern hemisphere, the moment when the first shoots of new growth start to break through the dark soil, drawn by the promise of sunlight.

> We breathe a new air,
> No longer cold with seeming death.
> The flowers respond
> to the strengthening Sun, your light.
> So may our hearts respond to your love and grace.
> The birds break into song and call us to your praise.
> So may our hearts give praise at all aspects of our lives.
> The frozen earth and water melt to new life:
> So may our hardened hearts be softened
> to gentleness and love.
> We are overwhelmed with images, symbols,
> confirmations of your resurrecting, your enlivening.

The year is swinging on its pivot and bringing us to the start of summer, celebrated on May 1 as the feast of Beltaine. Now that the light begins to overtake the dark the days lengthen and nights are shorter.

It was the time when the flocks would be taken from their winter quarters to graze and fatten in the high meadows throughout the summer. The people moved with their animals so that there was a regular transition. The farm names *hendre* and *hafod*, found throughout the area, refer to these winter and summer farms respectively, so that the landscape still carries a reminder of the yearly pattern of transition.

If Imbolc is the season of light, Beltaine is the season of growth, and prayer becomes praise for fulfillment:

> Strong image of your creative power.
> Calling forth the endless variety of your creative
> Imagination:
> Colour, scent and sound.
> Making for Beauty
> And for peaceful Joy.

Finally, on August 1 the feast of Lammas marks the beginning of the harvest when the earth brings its fruits to birth. Because of the new pattern of the year dictated to us by school terms and holidays, which cut across the older and more natural rhythms of the seasons, the common assumption is to regard August as the height of summer, the time for seaside vacations, camping, journeys abroad. But I have found that to follow the Celtic sense of timing now feels much more convincing. For this is harvest time, the gathering in of the fruits, the time to celebrate the main subsistence crops, whether of the fields, the hedgerows, or the orchards—and not least the time for their storing, conserving, and preserving in whatever way is the most appropriate to each. Sadly, for many today, this process is disappearing, for the speed at which we live and the ease of frozen food have meant the loss of those earlier traditional skills that respected the unique character and quality of each thing as it came to ripen and be gathered and handled accordingly.

The Orthodox liturgy of the Transfiguration on August 6 ends with the blessing of the first fruits. This should be one of the most joyous times because the threshold of plenty has been crossed. So Philip Jebb prays:

> The flowers have turned to seeds and fruit,
> For our enjoyment,

Our sustenance,
And our future life.
This is the time of fulfillment and completion.
It had a beauty of its own:
Perfect symbol of your providence.
We rejoice in the fruits you give us
in your loving generosity.

3

Embracing Life's Changes

From birth to death

Can this theme of crossing the borders apply to the pattern of my own life? What about all those transitions that occur from birth to death? They are not generally marked by ritual apart from the three events for which today's society has fashionable social (and religious) gatherings: baptism, marriage, and death. Christenings, weddings, and funerals are ceremonies that reflect important public high moments, and this is absolutely right. But they do not help when I feel the need for something in addition, for some ritual that will recognize that in all our lives there is a succession of passing-over moments, many of which must remain secret and private.

The traditional worldview, entrenched into every African child's psyche, speaks of interrelated worlds, the world of the living and the world of the dead, together making one whole and complete community under God's direct control and influence. African people belong to these two worlds that overlap and inter-connect. They never forget the spirit world, the human being as part of a bigger system. They see Earth as a gift from God, the rendezvous of the dead and the living. They speak to us of what is fundamental, universal, and what all of us recognize as being part of that primal vision—to which we are heir—even though sometimes we have neglected it, and with God's grace need to reclaim.

In the *Carmina Gadelica* we see how, until quite recently, life in the Scottish highlands and islands had its rituals and blessings for every stage of the life of the household. Family members conducted the rituals in the home itself. From the moment of birth, the mother would make a distinction between the more formal clerical, or "great," baptism in church and the birth baptism over which she presided in the house. The newborn child would be passed three times across the hearth and then carried three times sunwise (the pattern of the sun's daily journey) around the hearth, ensuring its insertion into the natural rhythm and flow of the universe, and then finally three drops of water would be placed on the baby's head. Here are timeless, primal elements, powerful images that transcend our immediate experience.

Coming of age

I was reminded of just how powerful such rituals can, and perhaps should, be from my experience of Africa. In Zimbabwe, or Rhodesia as it was then, the ears of the young boys were pierced as the first step of initiation into manhood. A doctor whose family has long belonged there and who understands this rite tells us that this "opened" his ear to things of the spirit, and enabled him to listen properly to worldly matters and understand them, to listen with understanding more than just as a child. This is all part of that African sense of progress into knowledge: "I had to concentrate on how to know my inner self and how to use it; on how other people lived or thought; and how the intricacies of nature wove into a harmonious whole."[1]

While I was staying with the brothers of the Order of the Holy Cross in South Africa, a young man was going through the traditional initiation rites that mark the transition to manhood in his culture. He was in his hut on the edge of the property, and although of course I did not see him—all women are rigidly excluded during this time—I knew what was happening. Customs and traditions are firmly established in Xhosa tribal life, so that as a person moves from childhood to teenage years to adulthood to middle age and finally to old age, each step has its dress, its songs and dances. They believe that this age grouping brings stability to the social structure and establishes a succession of responsibilities and obligations. The young *umkhetha* was experiencing the initiation rite into manhood that was essentially based on circumcision, and involved exclusion from all tribal life until the cut healed. Then the young men would emerge with new clothes (particularly noticeable were the tweed caps) and with white clay on their faces, in public demonstration of their new status in society. Although this may seem far from any western experience, it gave me a powerful image. With the young men wrapped only in blankets, and in the simplicity of huts specially built of branches that would later be burned, this time of initiation required poverty and nakedness, or near nakedness. There is a sense of being re-born, divesting oneself, becoming a *tabula rasa* ready to be filled with the knowledge and wisdom of the tribe. It seemed to me that there was a parallel here with the novice, who on admission to the community lies prostrate on the ground, saying *Suscipe* me, accept me, receive me, here I am empty before God in order to receive.

There is this same almost physical quality in the blessing that the mother would give to the son or daughter who was leaving home:

Be the great God between thy two shoulders
To protect thee in thy going and in thy coming.

A ritual for letting a son or daughter go free, handing them over, under the protection of God, is not something that we naturally include as a part of growing up today in the west; yet we are here reminded of one of the most important steps of all of the transitions in life, moving from the confines of the family into freedom and maturity.

Death

As the time of death draws closer, there is this same sense of confidence in the abiding presence of a God who is alongside us and has walked every step of the way with us. Therefore, there is nothing remote or abstract in the blessings that, in their own words, are asked before "crossing the black river of death; the great oceans of darkness; and the mountains of eternity." For while a funeral is an event shared by family and friends, the time of dying is uniquely personal. Keeping watch beside the bedside of an old woman as she was dying, I found that these deathbed blessings, as I recited them time and again, had a sense of being outside of time, and their constant repetition enhanced their timeless quality. Many, as this one, have a strong sense of passage, and although ultimately that passing over from this life is made alone, those who have preceded us, the saints and the angels, are waiting to bring us to God.

> Be each saint in heaven,
> Each sainted woman in heaven,
> each angel in heaven
> Stretching their arms for you,
> Smoothing the way for you,
> When you go thither
> Over the river hard to see;
> Oh when you go thither home
> Over the river hard to see.[2]

If we begin to see the world in this way, then nightfall and sleep become reminders of that final crossing over, which will in the end bring us from sleep and death into light and life.

> Be this soul on Thine arm, O Christ,
> Thou King of the City of Heaven.[3]

Embracing change

If we are going to see life as a succession of thresholds to be crossed, we are reminded of the journeys of the people of Israel in the desert, and we then find symbols and images that we can apply to our own experience. The very words *passover* and *exodus* carry a fullness of meaning as a journey from bondage into freedom. It is important to remember that the passover was a yearly ritual, so that its memory was kept alive and the cycle lived through time and time again:

> As we sing our own song of Freedom
> by practicing the Art of Passingover
> . . . gradually the face of our life begins to change;
> it becomes face of freedom.[4]

The psalms are the journey songs of the people who made that passage. Time and again they raised a fist to God and shouted angrily at him, asking him where his will was in their lives. Had he forgotten or betrayed his faithful people? If we try to sanitize, edit, or sentimentalize the psalms, they lose their power. They are the songs of a people who were moving away from a known situation into the unknown, and they were often angry with a God who removed all those certainties, who instead seemed to be leading them along an apparently precarious path. They did not sit down for long beside gently flowing streams or linger in lush meadows. When we pray the psalms as they did, we, too, are compelled to stay "at the raw edge," in the words of Walter Brueggemann.[5]

In the Gospels we watch a Christ who, in dismissing certainties, shows us what freedom might mean. We watch the way in which he enters into people's lives and *dissolves* an existing situation, whatever it might be. The likelihood was that the condition had promised security, safety, but now Christ challenges the people to *leave* their nets, or to *leave* a nice safe booth, and follow him. He says to Peter, James, and John, "Come," and to Matthew, "Stand up, move, walk, come with me." Our God is a God who moves and he invites us to move with him. He wants to pry us away from anything that might hold us too securely: our careers, our family systems, our money making. We must be ready to disconnect. There comes a time when the things that were undoubtedly good and right in the past must be left behind, for there is always the danger that they might hinder us from moving forward and connecting with the one necessary thing, Christ himself.

When Brueggemann writes about the Jewish people at one historic point in their story, the sacking of Jerusalem and the loss of the temple in 597, he uses the word *relinquish*.[6] It becomes a metaphor for the opening up to the new gifts and new forms of life given by God that become possible just when everything seems to have come to an end. Of course there is loss and it is right to grieve and not to pretend otherwise. Insecurity makes certitude attractive, and it is in times like these that I want to harness God to my preferred scheme of things, for it is risky to be so vulnerable. Yet it is this vulnerability that asks for trust and hope in God's plans, not mine. So I try to learn each time that I am called upon to move forward to hand over the past freely, putting it behind me, and moving on with hands open and ready for the new.

In the garden Christ gently but deliberately says to Mary Magdalene, *"Noli me tangere"* "Do not touch" is a misleading translation that deprives us of the significance of what is happening here.

"Do not cling" is a more accurate rendering of the Greek, for surely we *do* need to touch, to touch the hem of the garment, to touch the wounds and feel them. But we must not *cling,* for that carries the danger of becoming dependent, of clutching or holding on in the wrong way. I love the statue of the Walking Madonna by Elisabeth Frink in the cathedral close at Salisbury. Here is this young woman who strides out boldly into the future, her one hand strong and determined, while the other is vulnerable. She knows that she has seen the Lord, the risen Christ; she has heard the resurrection message and now she is ready to cross the threshold and engage whatever lies before her.

What gives her the strength to move forward with today: such assurance, calling out that loving welcome, that *Deo Gratias,* to a future that is unsure, unknown?

Interlude: Crossing over with Saints and Angels

The barriers go down between this world and the next. Celtic blessings and rituals carry the African sense of "the living dead," an idea wonderfully expressed in this twentieth-century Welsh poem, suggesting St. David's presence on the soil of Wales today:

> There is no barrier between two worlds in the Church,
> The Church militant on earth

Is one with the Church triumphant in heaven,
And the saints are in this Church which is two in one.[1]

The saints accompany us on our journeys. The
angels move easily between heaven and earth.
There is constant crossing between two worlds.
"A hill touches an angel," in the words of Dylan
Thomas, a Welsh poet *par excellence,* and there are
more attributions to St. Michael with all his angels
in this area than in the rest of the country. Bucolic
angels smile from tombstones in the churchyard or
look down on us from funerary tablets on church
walls as we sit in the pew below them. In the priory
church at Abergavenny, the giant wooden figure
of Jesse lies on his side while the angel at his head
keeps watch:

The angel at his head is awake to see for him . . .
Jesse need not wake yet
With amazement, the angel
sees.[2]

The Rev. Francis Kilvert, the nineteenth-
century country parson and diarist who lived here
in the Welsh borders, came to know his people and

their local traditions well. In one of his parishes, he was told that the people used to gather on Easter morning "to see the sun dance and play in the water and the angels who were at the Resurrection playing backwards and forwards before the sun." They were not serving any useful purpose, as the local poet Ruth Bidgood tells us in her poem "Resurrection Angels," they were not there for healing, they were at play—and in their dancing and playing they touched something in each of the onlookers:

> To and fro went the wings, to and fro
> over the water, playing before the sun.
> . . .
> The people had no words to tell
> the astonishment, the individual bounty—
> for each his own dance in the veins,
> brush of wings on the soul.[3]

4

Connecting Inner and Outer

The inner cloister

In his book *Living on the Border of the Holy*, a.
title that is itself significant, William Countryman writes of that border country that we all carry
within us. He describes it as a kind of fault line that
runs right down the middle of our lives. We can of
course ignore it but it does not go away. We all live

with it and we all have our unique experience of it, for it is part of who we are as human beings. It connects the surface or the ordinary reality with its deeper roots; indeed, he would actually claim that the border country is the realm in which human existence finds its meaning:

> This border country is a place of intense vitality. It does not so much draw us away from the everyday world as it plunges us deeper into a reality of which the everyday world is like the surface.... To live there for a while is like having veils pulled away. In the long run we find that the border country is in fact the place we have always lived, but it is seen in a new and clearer light. Stay at the border, in active conversation with the holy and the everyday.[1]

If we now return to St Benedict's portrait of the porter waiting at the gates, we could almost say that this shows us a conversation between the holy and the everyday—between the inner enclosure with its life of prayer and the exterior world with all its distractions and demands. How do we hold the two together? How do we have a conversation and not a confrontation? The porter shows us what makes possible this strong, warm act of welcome. We see this figure of *stability,* someone who does not go wandering off, either literally or metaphorically. He is firmly rooted in this place, in himself. It is from this firm internal center that the external can be greeted and welcomed, however strange, even challenging, it might appear. The porter gives us the image of standing on the threshold between two worlds.

The demands of the enclosure, with its times of prayer and silence, ask for those qualities of commitment and continuity, which bring a strong underpinning not only to the Benedictine life but to any fulfilled and balanced life. The cloister itself gives us such an amazing image that I return to it time and again. What other complex of buildings has the audacity to put emptiness at its heart? It originates in the eighth century when the cloister and the church were established as the two essential elements of the monastic buildings. Since then it has taken many forms and variants, as in Namibia where the Tutsing Missionary Benedictine sisters have just built a cloister whose walkways open out at each of the four corners so that the community should never feel separated from the mountainside on which the monastery is built. To walk slowly around these four sides, whether they were built in Africa in the twenty-first century or in Europe in the Middle Ages, can tell us so much about how emptiness and stillness at the heart of life can be achieved.

These passageways play a practical purpose that is also symbolic. They link all those buildings that serve the daily needs of a life that recognizes the demands of body, mind, and spirit—the holding together of the physical self with its need for sleep and food (the dormitory and the refectory); the self of the mind (the library where the intellect comes into play, and the chapter house where matters of day-to-day administration, finance, and business are handled, requiring the use of the intelligence); and finally the spiritual self (the church or the oratory). In the end, one might say that this whole balance of the three elements is actually dependent on the church, for it is the time and place for prayer that is the one essential priority that anchors everything else. Sleeping, eating, studying, manual work, decision making—all these other activities flow in and out of the work of God, the *opus Dei*. Prayer is the unifying foundation that maintains everything else in equilibrium. Muddle, confusion, being pulled first in one direction and then another, militate against a life with any sense of rhythm or unity. But here we see how living—however busy daily work may be—and praying can now become one continuous flowing movement, so that life is whole, a unified whole, in which no one thing is set above or apart from another.

Around that central open space run the arches, the succession of columns or pillars that carries the inner sides of the cloister walkways. Constantly changing according to the times of the day, the seasons of the year, they present us with a variety of amazingly varied and beautiful shadow patterns. Would there be the same perspective without these shadows? That is a good question to ask. It brings me back to the earlier theme of the light and the dark and the interplay of the two.

A gardener who traveled widely to write a book on monastic gardens was struck by the cloister garth, or garden, of this central space, open to the heavens, tunneling daylight into the heart of the monastery. He noticed how often members of a community liked to sit in the cloister at twilight, reading by the last rays of daylight before Compline. He reflected on the importance of the presence of light, together with the presence of the green of grass and flowers, and above all the fountain or spring that brings a quiet and continuous undercurrent of sound to the whole:

> Living in a building with good light is mentally uplifting. . . . The setting of green grass within the cloister range has long been known to have a unique power and grace and to exert a kind of subliminal attraction . . . cloister garths create green oases of safety, simplicity, and purity.[2]

As I apply these comments to my own inner self, I am reminded of the importance of keeping a garden watered and fresh throughout all the differing times of the day and the changing seasons of the year. For it is the water in the center that furnishes the most significant image; it is the refreshment of the spring of living water that keeps the garden green and gives it life.

Passing over and coming back

There are so many ways of describing this still center: the cave of the heart, the hidden poustinia, the innermost cloister. Each one of us has our own picture. Essentially it is that deep place where God finds us and we find him. It is not empty space *per se;* its purpose is to become the space for listening to the Word. We enter into silence and hear God's conversation and take our proper part in it—and if we heed ancient wisdom, that means trying not to say too much ourselves.

But it is the center from which we move outwards. Monastic men and women, Thomas Merton above all, describe themselves as people who are marginal, who are living on the edges, and yet they are also the most the profoundly centered. As I think about the center and the edges in my own life, I ask myself about the relationship of the two. Are the edges not perhaps the center? Does the center not hold the edges? Perhaps it is just simply finding the right connection of the two, the right way of coming and going.

If the borders are not frontiers, and if the thresholds are continually crossed and re-crossed, then we open up to the new. John Dunne reminds us that: "We all have this capacity to pass over and to come back again to ourselves, but we do not all discover it or learn how to use it." He then goes on to say: "I feel able to pass over into the other and come back again with new insights to my own."[3]

Encountering new worlds

At the very end of his Rule when St. Benedict encourages his followers, in an almost throwaway line, about the need to continue reading and studying, he makes suggestions about what he would like them to study. It is one of the best examples of being told about preparing to open up to the new. For the two main sources that he proposes are taken from almost diametrically opposing perspectives, very different in their approaches. To explore divergent forms of monastic experience was not going to be a comfortable exercise. Yet the man who is looking for the welcome of the open door and the open heart is also looking for the open mind. The porter welcomes the stranger, who may be a visiting monk; the brothers who take him in are also ready to listen to him. It may well be that this man comes from some different tradition, but they accept that they can learn from what he says. To listen to everyone, whoever they may be, brother, child, fellow professional, is important. I like to think of this exchange as conversation; it is gentler than the word dialogue, which often carries a sense of confrontation. *A Vow of Conversation* is the title that Thomas Merton gave to his journals for the years 1964–65 and in his case it also becomes a play on words.[4] He is referring to *conversatio morum,* the vow of conversion of manners, to continual conversion and ongoing transformation in the life of a Trappist monk. But it also describes the way in which this solitary hermit loved to receive that stream of visitors who came from all walks of life and every sort of religious, philosophical, literary background to talk with him and exchange ideas. His vow of stability brought him rootedness both in the Trappist community at Gethsemane and also more profoundly in his own inner self. It gave him the place from which his interior journey could begin—breaking open new worlds, asking new questions, and unveiling new vistas. In the last year of his life he wrote of the need for effort, deepening, change, and transformation. Not that I must undertake a special project of self-transformation or that I must "work on myself . . . let change come quietly and invisibly on the inside."[5]

5

The Time Between Times

When he spent time in Thomas Merton's hermitage, the journalist and racial rights activist John Howard Griffin learned much about himself and his situation from being alone, living in great simplicity, dependent on the coming and going of light and dark:

As you become more deeply attuned to the mystery of reality . . . it teaches you things you can hardly put into words, that can only be hinted by words, to abandon the self satisfaction of comfortable categories, to accept the unity of opposites (or contradictoriness) as the natural thing it is in reality.[1]

He found, as he knew that Merton did, that it was the times between times, and above all the hours before dawn that were the most significant part of this mystery of reality. Here is the first entry in his diary as he established himself in the place where he was hoping to complete his biography of his old friend:

August 6, 1969. 5:45 A.M. Before dawn.

With the beginnings of predawn-light some of the birds come to life—not with singing yet, but with a kind of murmuring. I carried my coffee out on the concrete porch and drank it walking back and forth. The air is cool, almost cold, and fresh. Light came slowly. I watched the trees assume black shapes through the fog. I thought of Tom who saw the sounds, smelled the same predawn freshness, allowed the same silences to do their work in him.[2]

"The darkness before dawn" is one of Griffin's favorite phrases as he himself begins the start of his day by waiting for the dawn, and finding what these hours can bring—"hours of the rarest happiness when the silence, the dripping of the rain, the popping of the fire, and the blackness of night become prayer, and you are just there involved in all of that, your whole being saying the wordless amens. . . ."[3] This was a time of "emptying out," of cleansing, of getting rid of all the junk in body, mind, and senses, and it brought him the truest and deepest sense of wholeness and interconnectedness.

This is the predawn time, but there is also the time at dusk as well, when the light fades, the "change-over routine" when evening falls, as I recalled earlier. This is particularly so in the winter: "the sun has disappeared. Dusk is near—utter stillness outside, grey snows, greyer skies . . . I watch the cold landscape turning towards night. . . . Long, long twilight. The light has scarcely dimmed outside, though some colour came into the sky through the woods to the west, a brilliant vermilion glow, startling in the greys . . . The moments of early dawn and late dusk are similar in the qualities of silence they evoke, and everything in me defers to them."[4]

For twilight, the time between times, brings true gray, the color that exists in its own right. Even the word itself, *twilight*, carries a gentle and lyrical sound, the time between lights, the greater light of the sun and the lesser light of the moon. Here is the moment of the changing of the guard between these two great luminaries. It is a fragile time of transition, half-light and half-dark—it is mysterious, ambiguous. It is the time of uncertainty, given to us daily as a reminder of the reality of the between-time.

It is an image from which we can learn so much, and it falls to the poet to tell us what this gift can mean. When Andrew Motion, the English Poet Laureate, was asked to turn the well-known English children's book *The Wind in the Willows* into a ballet libretto, he discovered an aura of mystery there that finds its way into these lines, spoken by the actor playing the author Kenneth Graham as he emerges into the attic and looks around him at the audience:

Here I am, just here. Awake
But dreaming. In the attic of my home—

> And nothing is quite certain any more.
> Is this grey twilight or the dusty air?
> You see? You can't be sure. And nothing's sure.
> Inside my head. I'm like a ghost that floats
> Between two worlds. . . .[5]

Recently when a nun in her mid-nineties sent me a note on my birthday, she quoted a line of Hegel: "The owl of wisdom flies in twilight" and then said, "I like to think that as we get older we live in two twilights; the evening twilight of letting-go and the dawn of looking forward. In both, Christ is our Light." This makes me think of "a kind of double vision in which we see both the light and the dark together and both sustain us," words actually taken from a book significantly entitled *Let Evening Come: Reflections on Aging*.[6]

Here is the giving up of the solace of certainty, for it means living with both/and. It is enjoying juxtaposition. It is embracing ambiguity. And if I recognize this poignant mix in my own inner landscape, ought I not let it shape my approach to the world around?

Each year we are given the chance to experience the power of the time between times, a reminder of the holiness of the pause, the space between. Yet it is generally neglected, misused. That most mysterious of all days, Holy Saturday, Easter Even, the day of Christ's descent into Hades is most usually one of decorating the church, preparing Easter lunch, getting ready for a vacation. A priest who drew back from all this parochial busyness and communal jollity wrote:

> Lord, they will scold me.
>
> Today I did not appear
> at the men's breakfast,
> the children's egg hunt.
> I dared not disturb
> this great silence
> with bacon or chocolates,
> the savory, sweet minutiae
> of parish life.
>
> Today I need,
> in simple solitude,
> to live Your absence,
> let it sweeten Your return,

make real Your presence
at tomorrow's festal feast.

This is the time of vital silence that gives meaning to the whole. It is like the silences in an orchestral performance that create the spaces between musical phrases and make the harmony possible. This same poet, Bonnie Thurston, reflects in her *Holy Saturday* the day on which "Nobody can be sure what will happen next."

I love this day
of silent waiting
when fasting is over,
but feasting not begun,
when pain is past
but flesh not quickened.
This is where we live,

this human place,
waiting before the cave
in the tarnished garden
where it all began
and ended

to begin anew,
we hope, forever.

This is where we live, she claims. But is it? To wait,
to keep vigil, to be ready with attentive listening?
She writes of the role of uncertainty:

Nobody can be sure
what will happen next.[7]

The costliness of being open

To be comfortable with uncertainty today requires
courage. Elsewhere I have written about asking
questions rather than finding answers, about
being content with hints and guesses, about the
importance of mystery. When I reflect on the
changes that I have witnessed in recent years in
South Africa, I see a country in which earlier
certainties have dissolved, for in the years of apartheid people were clearly ranged on either side
of issues; they knew where they stood, they had
banners and slogans and allies. Each side was
convinced of the morality of the stand they were
taking. Those in the expensive white suburbs

of Johannesburg did not venture into the black township of Soweto.

"We must try and make space for ambiguity." These words were said in the recent post-apartheid era by none other than Wilhelm Verwoerd, the grandson of the architect of apartheid—the "architect of Separate Development," Dr. Hendrick Verwoerd. Actjie Krog, in her powerful account of the *Truth and Reconciliation Commission,* which under Archbishop Desmond Tutu heard the testimonies of the victims of abuse and violence, tells how she once bumped into Wilhelm Verwoerd, the young philosophy professor. He smiled at her and said, "I had wanted to give you a quote: If truth is the main casualty in war, ambiguity is another. . . . One of the legacies of war is a habit of simple distinction, simplification and opposition. . . which continues to do much of our thinking for us." When her companion asked him what he meant by this he elaborated: "It means that in the past we had no choice but to live by simple white or black guidelines. But we shouldn't continue being dictated to by oversimplified credos during times of peace. We must try and make space for ambiguity."[8] Significantly, the final chapter of his autobiographical account of the change of heart that led to his joining the A.N.C. (the African National Congress, the spearhead of the struggle against apartheid) is entitled "A Commitment to Continuing Conversion."[9]

"We are not sinning if we are unsure of the answers to hard questions. We are sinning if we do not think or care." These are the words of that most wise and holy man Michael Ramsey. Perhaps this was unthreatening to him because this was how he lived, because he was himself familiar with this mysterious boundary between life now and life eternal, between experience and hope, between sorrow and joy. In 1966, when he was Archbishop of Canterbury, he wrote a small book called *Problems of Christian Belief in* which he spoke of the pattern of "alternating night and day" in his own life:

> Christian faith has been for me a constant process of wrestling, of losing and finding, of alternating night and day. For me the struggle is not between faith and unbelief so much as within faith itself. Faith is a sort of adventurous conflict in the midst of which certainty deepens. When the certainty passes, as it

does for me, into a sense of peace and serenity it is none the less a costly peace, a peace in the heart of conflict.[10]

Struggling with the challenge of the bitter tension and deep-rooted hatred that was breaking up society in Northern Ireland, a Methodist minister recently wrote of the inspiration and immediate implications he found as he reflected on the Trinity, not as a philosophical and speculative problem but as a practical experience to be lived:

In this vision of God there is real diversity in unity and unity in diversity. The three-one God is a community of mutuality, equality and reciprocity.... This vision of God critiques and challenges all our separatist, isolationist, sectarian division, and its exclusion and excluding zones. It calls us beyond the idea of benign apartheid or coexistence. Diversity in unity and unity in diversity, mutuality, equality, interdependence and interrelationships, are ultimate realities because they are of the very essence of God, who is Trinity.[11]

This is an encounter of hospitality in all its fullness. It is found in all traditional societies, and it is given very simple and profound expression in the portrait that St. Benedict draws in his Rule of the porter—on whom we are also to model ourselves, for this is his way of practical teaching. He shows us a man who stands at the gate, on the threshold of the monastery with the enclosure on one side and the world outside on the other. He welcomes those who come, no matter the time, and the reception he offers is loving, warm. It carries blessing: *Benedicite! Thanks be to God that you are here.* But true hospitality is one of both giving and receiving. As the well-known Benedictine writer Sr. Joan Chittister paraphrases it, "Thank God that someone has come to stretch our minds and souls. Thank God that someone has come to shake us out of our complacency. Thank God that someone has come to prod us beyond ourselves."[12]

Whatever name we may choose—the time between, the threshold, the pause—it is by naming it that we honor it and thereby honor change, movement, difference. When a book recently appeared in England written by the Chief Rabbi,

Jonathan Sacks, it was significantly given the title
The Dignity of Difference. In it Sacks wrote:

> Truth on earth is not, nor can it aspire to be, the
> whole truth. . . . God is greater than religion. . . . Can
> I recognise God's image in someone who is not in
> my image, whose language, faith, ideals are different
> from mine? If I cannot, then I have made God in
> my image instead of allowing him to remake me in
> his.[13]

He is telling us that God loves differences, as John
Habgood, the former Archbishop of York, wrote
when he was reviewing this book: "Human and
religious diversity is just as much in need of preser-
vation as biological diversity." After all, God called
a particular people in order to teach all people the
dignity of difference. "Babel was a terrible mistake,
not because God was in any way threatened by
human achievement, but because humanity, with
its newfound technological expertise, was attempting 'to impose a man-made unity on divinely
created diversity.'"[14]

  Listening means learning, and with that comes
the willingness to change. When the Jesuit William

Johnston lived in Japan, he began to listen to the voice of Buddhism, but because he was listening to two choruses he found he was beginning to ask questions. This was painful, for it opened up areas of consciousness that had previously lain dormant.[15]

The first step in listening, learning, and changing is to see that *different* is not dangerous; the second is to be happy and willing to live with uncertainty; the third is to rejoice in ambiguity and to embrace it. It all means giving up the comfort of certainty and realizing that uncertainty can actually be good. As soon as I realize this, I find that I must ask myself: what is my first task in approaching another people?

I have here set out my response as a meditation that is simultaneously also a form of prayer. It is inspired by something I saw pinned up in a Roman Catholic convent in Harare on a recent visit to Zimbabwe:

My first task in approaching another people
another culture
another religion
Is to take off my shoes.
For the place that I am approaching is holy.

> Otherwise I may find myself
> treading on another's dreams,
> their memories, their stories,
> More serious still—I might forget
> that God was there . . .

I need to pause, to take time, when I find myself on the threshold of another culture. I need to remind myself that as I meet them they will be bringing all their baggage of tradition and history, of suffering and triumph. So first I need to take time to look into my own self, to find in myself a willingness to be vulnerable, honest about my own story, its roots and its past, confronting the reality without attempting to escape into fantasy or nostalgia. For when I am attentive to where I am standing, I will also be attentive to where the other is standing, and only then will I be truly prepared to listen to them. There is nothing more important than this. It sounds so easy. Yet it is demanding, and essential, for it is fundamental, foundational. It means listening, the totality of listening, not only with the ears but also with the eyes.

This is something that we find portrayed so amazingly in the icon of the Rublev Trinity—and perhaps only the non-verbal could take us into the depths that we need. Here we see the visit of the three angels to Abraham, receiving his hospitality under the oak of Mamre—but also the three members of the Trinity sitting round the table with the cup in the center. The reverse perspective invites us all to enter and to partake of this company. We are not only observers, but also guests. We are drawn into this circle, we see those heads inclined toward one another, as they listen intently to each other, the hair drawn back so that the ear is exposed, as they look at one another "with listening eyes" as someone once commented. Each holds the other in a gaze of the most profound acceptance and love. This is the gaze of openness with nothing judgmental here, no rivalry, nothing obsessional— rather a look of gratitude and shared delight.

How far?

I have been writing this book at my cottage in the Welsh borders during the summer months, hoping to finish it by Lammas. I have gone constantly from my study to the orchard, the copse, the river- bank, taking with me my half-resolved thinking, and letting the rhythm between house and garden, inside and outside, work on me. Gardening in itself has about it something of this art of conversation. For my garden only exists through the "conversation" between myself and the given quality of the land itself in its natural state. I try to respect and enhance this without dominating. I try to do enough clearing, letting in enough light, and removing the destructive forces, to allow a continual exchange between myself and the natural elements. I hope that from this something will emerge that reflects a partnership between us. And since it is changing all the time, not only throughout the seasons but also year by year, as old trees die or floods alter the shape of the river banks, it will continue as an ongoing conversation in which both of us are involved. It is a reminder of border life.

Just as there is something unpredictable in life beside a stream—which continuously changes shape and configuration—as I come to the end of this exploration of the image of the border, I must also accept that it will not conclude with any clear-cut picture. But living with uncertainty is not the same as living with insecurity. It is important to differentiate the two. I know where I belong and am rooted, and with that firm base, that center, I can reach out, open up. Yet this inner space is not some closely guarded "sacred enclave," segregated and safely behind barriers, but a place open to growth and new life. I take to myself what Father Christian, the French Trappist monk in Algeria, wrote from his experience of living in a monastic community in a country where other cultures posed questions with which he had to engage. He was addressing the general chapter of the Cistercians in 1993, when he said these words, which really sum up where this book has been taking me: "Our Christian identity is always in the process of being born. It is a paschal identity."[16]

Certainty can appear immensely attractive, appealing both to individuals, and to nations above all, in times of suffering and distress. Complexity, ambiguity, untidiness—these are very different. I have come to find that they carry more conviction. The closed mind, the *laager* mentality, is the greatest obstacle to any real freedom—the freedom of openness. As soon as we admit that there are no right answers, that we must be ready to live with contradiction, we are forced instead to listen to one another, to admit our need to learn, to recognize our need to receive.[17]

> let us live with uncertainty
> as with a friend
> to feel certain
> means feeling secure.
> To feel safe is unreal,
> a delusion of self
> knowing we do not know is
> the only certainty letting the self be lost into Christ.

These words, written anonymously by a monastic, speak of the courage and strength that come from this way of living. It may be a brave, even a fool-hardy or risky undertaking, but if we choose to live on the borders we find ourselves part of a company of fellow travelers who are ready to say:

> For us there are no certainties, no star
> blazing our journey, . . .
> We try
> out our way lit with angels, wondering
> 'How far?'[18]

Perhaps there is something prophetic about living on the border. I want a Christianity that brings me comfort, but also *dis*-comfort. In the new science I find a vocabulary that, even if I do not fully understand it, helps me to articulate my own thoughts.[19] The old world of Newtonian certainty drew lines and was happy with whatever was systematic, rational, and could be subjected to reason. Now in a world of inter-relatedness, "connections work across the separations." "Senders and receivers" are linked together in a way that means energy, fertility, new birth. This is inevitably more complex and more demanding, just when I would like things to become smoother and simpler. Listening to other voices asks me not only to be attentive to the place where I stand and to ask questions of myself, but also to be open and willing to recognize where the other might bring in a corrective, a deepening or strengthening. Perhaps this will be painful, opening up areas of consciousness that previously were dormant. But in a two-way exchange the other has as much to give as I have to receive. Ideally the border should be the place of encounter and contrast that can lead, not to syncretism, but to a moving forward in greater fullness. It is a place that church and society have never needed more.

God, who is there at the center, is also at the raw edges. Our living God moves and expects us to move with him. God will not let us settle easily or for too long. Our God is too big for either/or. Instead he asks us to say both/and, so we move into that threshold to meet the God who is both known and unknown. The last pause of all is at the threshold of God who is unending mystery.

Notes

Introduction

1. Esther de Waal, *Lost in Wonder: Rediscovering the Spiritual Art of Attentiveness* (Collegeville, Minn.: Liturgical Press, 2003).

2. Graham Greene, *The Lawless Roads* (London: Penguin Books, 1939), 19.

3. L. William Countryman, *Forgiven and Forgiving* (Harrisburg, Pa.: Morehouse Publishing, 1998), 1–2.

4.   Paul Hill, "The Art of David Jones," in *David Jones* (London: Tate Gallery Publications Departments, 1991), 24.

1. The Border Landscape

1.   David Jones, *Epoch and Artist* (London: Faber, 1959), 251.

2.   R. S. Thomas, *Collected Poems 1945–1990* (London: Phoenix, 1993), 207. Permission sought.

3.   Bonnie Thurston, *The Heart's Lands* (Abergavenny: Three Peaks Press, 2001), 33. Professor Thurston has lectured in theology for over twenty-five years and written widely on New Testament studies. This poem and others on Herefordshire are the result of time spent here on the borders. Permission sought.

4.   This is the underlying theme of so much that I have written on the role of order in the Benedictine and Cistercian traditions.

5.   *A History of the Benedictine Priory of the Blessed Virgin Mary and St. Florent at Monmouth* (Aberystwyth: Cambrian Printers, 2001).

2. Times and Seasons or Crossing Between Light and Dark

1. David Scott, *Sacred Tongues: The Golden Age of Spiritual Writing* (London: SPCK, 2001), 6.

2. There is now a great deal of interesting material on the map. The best short introduction is that of Meryl Jancy, *Mappa Mundi: A Brief Guide* (Hereford: Hereford Cathedral Enterprises, 1995).

3. Leo the Great.

4. See selections from Alexander Carmichael's *Carmina Gadelica* in Esther de Waal, ed., *The Celtic Vision: Prayers, Blessings, Songs, and Invocations from the Gaelic Tradition* (Jefferson, Mo.: Ligouri/ Triumph, 2001). Originally published in London by Darton, Longman & Todd, 1988. All quotations from Celtic sources that follow can be found in full in this anthology that I published in order to make them easily accessible. This is taken from page 151.

5. John Davies, *God at Work: Creation Then and Now—a Practical Exploration* (Norwich: Canterbury Press, 2001), 12.

6.   Douglas Dales, *Christ the Golden Blossom: A Trea-sury of Anglo-Saxon Prayer* (Norwich: Canterbury Press, 2001), 17.

7.   Quoted from George Mackay Brown. Source unknown.

8.   Brigid Boardman and Philip Jebb, *In a Quiet Garden: Meditations and Prayerful Reflections* (Stratton on the Fosse: Downside Abbey Books, 2000). All of the quotations that I have used in this section are taken from the section on the seasons, 82–88. Quoted with permission.

3. Embracing Life's Changes

1.   Robert W. Fynn, *The Lost Bone* (London: Avon Books, 1996), 20–21.

2.   The comments were given to Alexander Carmichael as he collected these death blessings. See Esther de Waal, ed., *The Celtic Vision: Prayers, Blessings, Songs, and Invocations from the Gaelic Tradition* (Jefferson, MO: Liguori/ Triumph, 2001), 133.

3.   Ibid., 66.

4.   Francis Duff, *The Art of Passingover* (New York: Paulist Press, 1988), 153.

5.   Walter   Brueggemann,   *Hopeful   Imagination:
     Prophetic Voices in Exile* (Philadelphia: Fortress
     Press, 1986).

6.   Ibid.

Interlude: Crossing over with Saints and Angels

1.   D. Gwenallt Jones, "St. David." For the full text see
     pages 39–41 in *Daily Readings from Prayers and
     Praises in the Celtic Tradition* (ed. A. M. Allchin
     and Esther de Waal; Springfield, Ill.: Templegate
     Publishers, 1986).

2.   Ruth   Bidgood,   *Singing   to   Wolves*   (Seren:
     Poetry Wales Press, 2000), 29. Quoted with
     permission.

3.   Ruth Bidgood, *Selected Poems* (Seren: Poetry of
     Wales Press, 1992), 34. Quoted with permission.

4. Connecting Inner and Outer

1.   L. William Countryman, *Living on the Border of
     the Holy: The Human Priesthood and the Church*
     (Harrisburg, Pa.: Morehouse Publishing, 1999).

2. Mick Hales, *Monastic Gardens* (New York: Stewart, Tabori & Chang, 2000), chap. 1, "The Cloister Garth," 14–30.

3. John Dunne, *The House of Wisdom* (London: SCM Press, 1985).

4. The art of conversation is not only gentler but it is an art that can be learned. I am grateful to William Countryman for clarification on this small but important point. He helped to put my own experience into clearer perspective, op. cit, 205, note 27; 204, note 26. *A Vow of Conversation* was published in Basingstoke, England, by the Lamp Press in 1988.

5. Thomas Merton, *Woods, Shore, Desert: A Notebook, May 1968* (Santa Fe: Museum of New Mexico Press, 1982), 48.

5. The Time Between Times

1. John Howard Griffin, *The Hermitage Journals:, A Diary Kept While Working on the Biography of Thomas Merton* (ed. Conger Beasley, Jr.; Garden City, N.Y.: Image Books, 1983), 49.

2. Ibid., 1.

3. Ibid., 47–48.

4. Ibid., 73.
5. This is taken from an article in *The Guardian* 17.02.02.
6. Mary Morrison, *Let Evening Come: Reflections on Aging* (New York: Doubleday, 1998), 139.
7. These are unpublished poems by Bonnie Thurston and I am grateful to her for allowing me to include them here.
8. Antjie Krog, *Country of My Skull* (Johannesburg, South Africa: Random House, 1998), 99.
9. Wilhelm Verwoerd, *My Winds of Change* (Randburg, South Africa: Ravan Press, 1997).
10. Douglas Dales, Glory: *The Spiritual Theology of Michael Ramsey* (Norwich: Canterbury Press, 2003). The quotations given in this paragraph come successively from pages 46, 15, and 5.
11. Johnston McMaster, "Celtic Resources for a Peace Process," in *Celtic Threads: Exploring the Wisdom of Our Heritage* (ed. Padraigin Clancy; Dublin: Veritas, 1999), 96–98.
12. This is taken from an article written for *Benedictine Bridge: The Journal of the Sisters of St. Benedict* (Madison, Wis.: Advent, 2000). In 1992, the Roman Catholic Sisters of St. Benedict of Madison, Wisconsin, began a visionary process that has led

to anew ecumenical monastic community following the Rule of St. Benedict. It is the first of its kind
in North America.

13. Jonathan Sacks, *The Dignity of Difference: How
to Avoid the Clash of Civilizations* (London: The
Continuum Publishing Group, 2003).

14. I am quoting here from a review article by John
Habgood that appeared in the Anglican weekly
newspaper *The Church Times.*

15. See William Johnston, *Mirror of the Mind* (London:
Collins Fount, 1981), 10–11,14.

16. See John W. Kiser, *The Monks of Tibhirine: Faith,
Love, and Terror in Algeria* (New York: St. Martin's
Press, 2002).

17. See Esther de Waal, *Living with Contradiction: An
Introduction to Benedictine Spirituality* (Harrisburg, Penn.: Morehouse Publishing, 1997).

18. Sr. Jennifer Dines, *A Touch of Flame: An Anthology
of Contemporary Christian Poetry* (comp. Jenny
Robertson; London: Lion Paperbacks, 1989), 25.

19. I have gained much from reading Margaret
Wheatley, *Leadership and the New Science: Discov-
ering Order in a Chaotic World* (San Francisco:
Bennett-Koehler Publishing, 1999), 28.